Dream Makers on the Nile

First published in Egypt in 1998 by
The American University in Cairo Press
113 Sharia Kasr al Aini
Cairo, Egypt.

All photographs are from the archives of Muhammad Husayn Bakr; except the photographs of Togo Mizrahi and Kamal Selim, courtesy of Dar al-Hilal archives.

Copyright text © 1998 Zeitouna. All rights reserved.

No part of this publication may be reproduced, stored in a retrieval system or transmitted in any form or by any means, electronic, mechanical, photocopying, recording or otherwise, without the prior written permission of the copyright owner and the publisher.

Dar el Kutub No. 11802/96
ISBN 977 424 429X

Printed in Egypt

Dream Makers on the Nile

A Portrait of Egyptian Cinema

by
Mustafa Darwish

A Zeitouna Book
The American University in Cairo Press

Contents

Foreword	7
Introduction	9
Muhammad Karim	15
Togo Mizrahi	16
Ahmed Badrakhan	17
Muhammad Abd al-Wahab and Umm Kulthum	18
Kamal Selim	19
Naguib al-Rihani	20
Ismail Yasin	21
Amina Rizk	22
Yusef Wahbi	23
Layla Murad	24
Anwar Wagdi	25
Farid al-Atrash and Asmahan	26
Tahiya Karioka	27
Asya, Ahmed Galal, and Marie Queenie	28
Henry Barakat	29
Fatin Hamama	30
Omar al-Sharif	31
Abd al-Halim Hafez	32
Na'eema Akef	33
Suad Husni	34
Rushdi Abaza	35
Salah Abu Sayf	36
Kamal al-Shaykh	37
Tawfik Saleh	38
Niyazi Mustafa	39
Hassan al-Imam	40
Fatin Abd al-Wahab	41
Shadi Abd al-Salam	42
Yusef Chahine	43
Supporting Stars	44

Foreword

This book deals with the Egyptian film industry in its formative period. Starting at the beginning of the twentieth century, this period ended in the early 1960s with the wave of nationalization that made the public sector cinema's guardian, or perhaps its jailer.

The book is made up of biographical sketches of the greatest figures in Egyptian cinema—directors, actresses, and actors—whose contributions were breakthroughs for the growing industry.

A section of movie stills is devoted to the period's supporting stars, whose roles were often of enormous and enduring importance. Taken together, these sketches and photographs are intended to present a portrait of the glory days of Egyptian cinema.

The Arabic titles of films are given when they first appear in any section, followed by a translation, which is used thereafter. Some titles are personal names—for example, *Layla, Imtithal*—and therefore need no translation.

Publicity for Ghazal al-Banat (*The Flirtsation of Girls*, 1951) directed by Anwar Wagdi.

The first showing of a film in Egypt took place on 5 November 1896 in one of the halls of Tusun Pasha in Alexandria. Later in the same month another was shown in Cairo, in the hall of Hamam Schindler near the old Shepheard's Hotel. Not even a year had passed since the art was born in Paris on 28 December 1895.

In this, as in so much else in Egypt's history, geography played its crucial part. Standing between East and West, between Europe and Asia, and holding together the eastern and western flanks of the Arab world, Egypt at the end of the nineteenth century was a meeting place and a melting pot. Here the transplanted culture of a rapidly changing Europe met with the philosophies and cultures of the East. At the same time, eastern Arabs, from Palestine, Syria, and Mount Lebanon, settled in Egypt and founded newspapers, publishing companies, theater troupes, and commercial enterprises. The result was a cultural renaissance, in which cinema, blending the language of modernity and the spirit of ancient Egyptian wall painting, was to thrive. Evidence of the early grip of cinema on the Egyptian psyche is provided by writer Yahya Haqqi, recalling his childhood in the first decade of the century:

> *I was raised in a family that was in love with the cinema, young and old alike. Dinnertime conversation never left the subject of old films, current films, and films that were yet to come; the names of actors in Italy, Germany, and America, and comparisons between them. I was always waiting impatiently for Thursday because it was the only day I was permitted to go to the theater and watch films, and I would look forward to it all week, starting on Friday morning, counting the days and the hours, wanting a whole lifetime to pass in the blink of an eye.*

Haqqi's memories are of foreign films. Indigenous Egyptian cinema was still a dream—in the view of some, an impossible dream. In the early years, for all Egypt's great love of cinema, importing the necessary equipment, building studios, and equipping theaters was well nigh impossible. The first quarter of cinema's life on the banks of the Nile yielded only short films on events like the funeral of the nationalist leader Mustafa Kamel (8 August 1909), or the official departure of the Hajj caravan to the Hijaz (October 1912), and even these were made by foreigners or naturalized foreigners.

The first Egyptian film actor was Muhammad Karim, who appeared in *Sharaf al-Badawi* (Honor of the Bedouin, 1918), then in *al-Azhar al-Moumita* (Deadly Flowers, 1918), which the censors refused to license for the general public. Both films were made by an Italian production company, which then ceased operations and sold its equipment to Alfizi Orfanelli, also Italian and the cinematographer for *Madame Loretta* (1919), directed by Leonardo Larizzi. In *Madame Loretta*, Fawzi al-Gazairli became the first Egyptian to take a leading role on the screen.

In 1920 a documentary was made of the funeral of nationalist leader Muhammad Farid, and then a short feature film, *The American Aunt*, inspired by the play *Charley's Aunt*. The lead in this film was given to Ali al-Kassar, a famous theatrical star, who played the role of a man disguised as a woman.

Three years later Muhammad Bayumi returned from Germany, where he had been studying cinematography. Bayumi was the first Egyptian to produce and shoot a newsreel, *Amun*, which is the only cinematic record of the return

Husayn Sidki and Fatima Rushdi in al- Azima (1939).

from exile in 1923 of the nationalist leader Saad Pasha Zaghlul. Bayumi was also the first Egyptian to shoot a fiction film, *Fi Ard Tutankhamun* (In the Land of Tutankhamun, 1923), produced and directed by Victor Rossitto, a Cairene lawyer of Italian origin. Bayumi then became the first Egyptian to both direct and shoot a short fiction film, *al-Bashkateb* (The Head Clerk, 1924), which he made for LE 100. Just thirty minutes long, the film revolves around a clerk who becomes involved with a dancer, embezzles money, and ends up in prison, a theme to be repeated in many a film over the next seventy years.

In 1927 Aziza Amir produced and acted in a long feature film she called *Layla,* the first of its kind to be financed by Egyptian capital. The film was first shown at the Metropole Theater in Cairo, and Aziza Amir was given a standing ovation. "I hope this crescent turns into a beautiful full moon," said Ahmed Shawqi, the Prince of Poets. Talat Harb, founder of Banque Misr and a far-sighted builder of Egypt's modern economy, expressed his admiration by telling Amir she had accomplished what men could not. *Al-Ahram* newspaper waxed lyrical. Why, it asked, could Egypt not in a few years build a city like Hollywood, in Imbaba, northwest of Cairo? With this film, the editorial went on, Amir had initiated the project of giving life to a cinema in

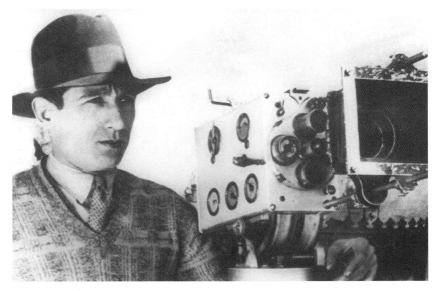

Above: Muhammad Karim. Below: Studio Misr

Egypt. "Imbaba will compete with Hollywood," it said. "May God make these hopes come true."

Talat Harb refused to be carried away by this flood of enthusiasm. Seven months before, he had given a speech at a showing of some short documentary films produced by his Misr Acting and Cinema Company. "The cinema industry", he said, "is extremely multifaceted. It would be wise for us to proceed gradually, so that once we have mastered some of the more simple elements of the process we can then move to more complex structures. Ultimately we will reach the point of making and projecting fiction films. But it is not our intention at this point to produce such films, or to show them, because while fiction films may be the most powerful element in the life of the cinema, we must not bite off more than we can chew."

In keeping with this philosophy, it was not until 1936 that Talat Harb gave the green light for his studio to produce a long feature film. In the intervening period, Egyptian studios produced forty-four films, harbingers of the great development that was still to come.

The influence of director Muhammad Karim was felt with his first film, *Zaynab* (1930), adapted from a novel by Muhammad Husayn Haykal Pasha. Karim's *Awlad al-Zawat* (Children of the Aristocracy, 1932) was the first Egyptian talkie or, more accurately, half-talkie. It was also the first film in which stage actors Yusef Wahbi and Amina Rizq appeared. In 1933 Karim directed the first musical, *al-Warda al-Bayda'* (The White Rose), featuring Muhammad Abd al-Wahab.

Further important developments came with figures like Ibrahim and Badr Lama, Asya, Mary Queenie, Ahmed Galal, Naguib al-Rihani, Togo Mizrahi, Fatima Rushdi, and Bahiga Hafiz. These names represent the end of a period in which Egyptian cinema was struggling to find a voice. The new age began with *Widad* (1936), the first long feature film made by Talat Harb's Studio Misr, which over the next thirty years was to produce some of the very best Egyptian films.

Widad marked a turning-point. A remarkable industry now began to grow in the face of some tremendous obstacles: an uncommon and persistent tendency to oversimplify, favoring quantity over quality; censorship with its three taboos—politics, religion, and sex; the nationalization of studios and theaters in the 1960s; and the decline of theaters when confronted with television, which the state supported. Nationalization and television together forced the submission of the moving image to the public sector, an ineffective, inefficient dinosaur marked by excess labor, accumulating debt, and the squandering of public funds.

In the face of all this, Egyptian cinema managed to resist annihilation, and indeed to thrive. It has spread the Cairene dialect throughout the Arabic-speaking world and made a sizeable contribution to world film production. If many films are derivative of other traditions, some, like Shadi Abd al-Salam's *al-Mummiya* (The Mummy, 1969), are truly original. Egyptian cinema survives through the vitality of its best film makers, and because over the years it has won the hearts of the Egyptian people, and fed their dreams.

Muhammad Karim (1896—1972)

Muhammad Karim was a pioneer of Egyptian cinema: the first to act in a film; the first to direct a film adapted from an Egyptian novel; the first to make a talkie; director of all Muhammad Abd al-Wahab's films; and toward the end of his career, the first dean of the Cinema Institute. Plenty to earn him the title Sheikh of Directors.

In the early 1920s, Karim traveled to Rome and Berlin. In Berlin, he watched German director Fritz Lang making *Metropolis* at UFA Studios. Of this experience, he wrote: "I went to Fritz Lang and asked permission to attend the whole production and enter the studio at any time. The man graciously gave me permission. When they learned at UFA Studios that I was studying film making, they gave me every assistance to learn first hand. Filming *Metropolis* required managing fifteen manually-operated cameras simultaneously; my friends allowed me to look through the lens from every angle. I was amazed at the precision of the work and took notes of everything as if I was at a great university. But could a university offer such an experience? When I say I am a graduate of *Metropolis*, I mean the year I spent among its workers at UFA Studios learning the art and craft of directing."

Returning to Egypt in 1926, Karim directed a short documentary, *Hada'iq al- Hayawan* (The Zoological Gardens, 1927) for Misr Acting & Cinema Company. With the financial backing of his close friend Yusef Wahbi, Karim directed his first silent feature film *Zaynab* (1930) and the first Egyptian talkie, *Awlad al-Zawat* (Children of the Aristocracy, 1932). His reputation was established.

A meeting was soon arranged between Karim and the great singer Muhammad Abd al-Wahab, at a party in the country home of prominent journalist Fikry Abaza. The film that emerged from that encounter, *al Warda al-Bayda'* (The White Rose, 1933), marked the beginning of a long and exclusive relationship. Karim became known as Abd al-Wahab's private director. From 1933 until 1944, he made only Abd al-Wahab films, and his attempts to break away by making films with other stars, brought scant success.

Togo Mizrahi (1905—1986)

Togo Mizrahi, with a Ph.D in economics, and fluent in several languages, was an immensely productive figure in Egypt's early cinema. In sixteen years he made thirty-two films, as director, author, scriptwriter, set designer, and sometimes actor. Between 1930 and 1946 he worked with every new aspect of film, making social dramas, musicals, and historical and heritage films, with a particular penchant for themes from *A Thousand and One Nights*.

Mizrahi's first film, *Kokayeen* (Cocaine, 1930) was made at his private studio in Alexandria, where it was first shown under the title *al-Haweya* (The Abyss). It was not until 1938 that he moved to Cairo and rented Studio Wahbi as his headquarters and production base.

In his early years, following the custom prevalent at the time for a Jewish actor to adopt a screen name that was common to the three main religions of Egypt, Mizrahi changed his name to Ahmed Mishriki. But the new identity was not to last long. In 1934 he released the first of four films that featured an unambiguously Jewish character, Shalom. *Al-Mandouban* (The Two Representatives, 1934) was followed by *Shalom al-Dragoman* (Shalom the Dragoman, 1935), *Shalom al-Riyadi* (Shalom The Athlete, 1937) and *al-Ezz Bahdala* (Prosperity is an Insult, 1937).

Mizrahi cast Ali al-Kassar, Egypt's famous black actor, in the leading role of nine of his films, notably *Alf Layla wa Layla* (A Thousand and one Nights, 1941), *Ali Baba wal-Arba'een Harami* (Ali Baba and the Forty Thieves, 1942), and *Nur al-Din wal-Bahara al-Thalatha* (Nur al-Din and the Three Sailors, 1944). Singer Layla Murad was also brought into cinema by Mizrahi, and appeared in five of his films, ending with *Layla fil-Zalam* (Layla in the Darkness, 1944).

In 1946 came *Sallama*, one of the most important films Mizrahi made before leaving Egypt. Inspired by Arab history, with lyrics by Bairam al-Tonsy, music by Zakariya Ahmed, and a fast pace, the film was a major success and was Umm Kulthum's best acting performance.

Soon after the release of *Sallama*, Mizrahi was accused of zionism and forced out of Egypt. He died in exile in Italy.

Ahmed Badrakhan (1909—1969)

As a student at law school, Ahmed Badrakhan decided to devote his life to the art he had adored since childhood. He corresponded with the Cinema Institute in Paris, and had articles on cinema published in *al-Sabah* magazine. Eventually he became the film editor of *al-Sabah* and abandoned completely the study of law.

In 1933, the industrialist Talat Harb asked Badrakhan to prepare a report on the cost of building a studio to produce talking films. Impressed with the report, Harb sent Badrakhan to study film making in France.

When he returned to Egypt at the end of 1934 to take up the post of director at Talat Harb's recently completed Studio Misr, Badrakhan brought with him a script he had written, a love story about a slave girl, Widad, and her master. However, Badrakhan had hardly completed filming the first few scenes of *Widad*—the studio's first film and the first to feature Umm Kulthum—than a conflict arose between him and the manager of the studio, Ahmed Salem. Badrakhan was replaced as director of *Widad* by Fritz Kramp, the studio's German technical director, and resigned.

By 1937, Badrakhan had directed Umm Kulthum's second film, *Nashid al-Amal* (Anthem of Hope) for another new company, Films of the East. *Nashid al-Amal* was distinguished by Badrakhan's seamless integration of the songs into the dramatic flow of the film. When Talat Harb saw it, he rebuked Ahmed Salem and invited Badrakhan to return to Studio Misr. Badrakhan took up the offer, but the musical he made on his return, *Shay' min la shay'* (Something from Nothing, 1938), flopped.

His second film with Umm Kulthum, *Dananir* (1940), is a landmark in Egyptian cinema. Following its release Badrakhan became known as Umm Kulthum's director, just as Muhammad Karim was Muhammad Abd al-Wahab's director. Badrakhan directed four of Umm Kulthum's six films—*Anthem of Hope, Dananir, Aida* (1943) and *Fatima* (1947)—in addition to the script and scenes he had directed of *Widad*.

After *Dananir,* he made his first non-musical, *Hayat al-Zalam* (Life of Darkness, 1940), a social melodrama, but quickly returned to musicals with *Intisar al-Shabab* (The Triumph of Youth, 1940), the first film to feature Farid al-Atrash and Asmahan.

Badrakhan's forty-one films made over thirty-two years are overwhelmingly romantic: *Laylat Gharam* (Night of Passion, 1951) and *'Ahd al-Hawa* (Time of Love, 1955) are perfect examples. But there were other films too. He made three patriotic films: a biography of nationalist leader *Mustafa Kamel* (1952); *Allah Ma'ana* (God is With Us, 1955) about events surrounding the Free Officers' movement; and a biography of the composer *Sayed Darwish* (1966). For eight years (1958—66), he stopped making films, then returned to make four more. He died just hours before the first showing of his last film, *Nadia* (1969).

Muhammad Abd al-Wahab (1897–1991) & Umm Kulthum (1904–1975)

From the beginning, Umm Kulthum and Muhammad Abd al-Wahab were competitors in everything musical in Egypt. By the 1920s their singing careers were in full swing. Abd al-Wahab was the Singer of Kings and Princes, Umm Kulthum the Star of the East.

Cinema attracted them both, and though Abd al-Wahab arrived first, it was inevitable that they should be competitors in cinema, just as they were in the recording industry. Abd al-Wahab's first film, *al-Warda al-Bayda'* (The White Rose), appeared in 1933, and was followed in 1936 by Umm Kulthum's *Widad*, the first full-length feature film made by Talat Harb's Misr Acting and Cinema Company and . For her role in *Widad*, Umm Kulthum received the very considerable some of LE5,000.

Clearly there was money to be made in films. Abd al-Wahab decided to produce his own, while Umm Kulthum continued to command high fees for her appearances. Ever competitive, they made almost the same number of films: Abd al-Wahab appeared in seven, ending with *Lastu Malakan* (I am not an Angel, 1946), and Umm Kulthum played in six, ending with *Fatima* in 1947.

Abd al-Wahab's films all had contemporary settings. Umm Kulthum's *Nashid al-Amal* (Anthem of Hope, 1937), *Aida* (1942), and *Fatima* were contemporary stories, but she also made historical films: *Widad, Dananir* (1940), and *Sallama* (1945) were set in the early days of Islam and the Abbasid empire.

Abd al-Wahab composed his own songs and also those of his leading ladies: Nagat Ali in *Dumu' al-Hubb* (Tears of Love, 1935); Layla Murad in *Yahya al-Hubb* (Long Live Love, 1938); and Ragaa Abdu in *Mamnu' al-Hubb* (Love is Forbidden, 1942). The three great composers of Umm Kulthum's film songs were Zakariya Ahmed, Riyad al-Sumbati, and Muhammad al-Qasabgi.

Abd al-Wahab devoted a good deal of energy to discovering promising female vocalists to sing in his films. In part this was due to the perceived decline in his own voice. around this time. Umm Kulthum's voice, on the other hand, was stronger than ever and with only a few exceptions she sang alone. In *Aida*, Ibrahim Hamuda also sang, and in *Widad* Umm Kulthum shared "In the Country of My Love." Soon after, however, she sang the song alone on record, and made it a hit.

Kamal Selim (1913–1945)

Kamal Selim was the director of *al-Azima* (Determination, 1939), probably the most famous of all Egyptian films.

Selim's father, who owned a silk shop, died while the boy was still in secondary school. As the eldest son, the family required him to succeed his father in business. However, his love of the cinema and his fascination with Rudolph Valentino changed the course of his life. Deserting the family, he fled abroad, hoping to study cinema in France. When the French president was assassinated a few days after Selim landed in Marseilles, he was deported back to Egypt.

He studied film magazines, watched movies, and tried unsuccessfully to get a scholarship through Talat Harb's Banque Misr. He played a desperate man in a film called *Ibtisamat al-Shaytan* (The Devil's Smile), and after a lot of nagging, the owner of Odeon Record Company commissioned him to direct *Wara' al-Sitar* (Behind the Curtain, 1937), costarring singers Abd al-Ghani al-Sayed and Ragaa Abdu. The film was poor and commercially unsuccessful, although the songs became very popular. It did however give Selim an entry to Studio Misr as a scriptwriter.

After writing the script for *al-Doktor* (The Doctor, 1939), Selim persuaded the studio to let him direct a film based on his own script. The film was to be called *Fil-Hara* (In the Alley) but he soon changed the title to *al-Azima*. An instant success, its name was to become a household word. *Al-Azima* was the first Egyptian film to deal with social issues that affected ordinary people. Although the plot was somewhat simple and naive, the action took place in a realistic setting, an alley inhabited by average, working-class people.

Contrary to expectations, the next film, *Ila al-Abad* (Forever, 1941), was technically poor and a commercial failure. Indeed Selim was never to make another film that even approached the quality of *al-Azima*. While preparing *Layla Bint al-Fuqara'* (Layla Daughter of the Poor), he died suddenly, aged just thirty-two.

Naguib al-Rihani (1892–1949)

Naguib Elias al-Rihani was born in Cairo of an Iraqi father and an Egyptian Coptic mother. A fan of acting since his school days, he eventually took his baccalaureate and was employed at the Agricultural Bank. It was there that he met Syrian director Aziz Eid. He quit his job at the bank, and worked instead with Eid, as an extra at the Opera.

When Eid formed his first theater company, al-Rihani quickly joined. When in the summer of 1915, Eid formed the Arab Comedy Troupe, al-Rihani again joined. There he learned the art of directing and was introduced to the French farce that would be a major influence on his own brand of comic theater.

He did not remain long with the troupe as disputes broke out between him and Eid, especially on the subject of adaptation. Eid thought an adapted play should be completely faithful to the French original. Al-Rihani believed it should be compatible with Egyptian taste. "We want an Egyptian theater with the smell of ta'ameya and moloukheya not boiled potatoes and beefsteak!" said al-Rihani.

With this attitude, he created the most famous comic duo in Egyptian comedy, Kishkish Bey and his attendant Zorob. Kishkish Bey, the mayor of Kafr al-Balas, embodied the contradictions between village and city ethics.

Kishkish Bey also brought al-Rihani fame and wealth. He formed his own theater company, and produced his first play, *Hamar wa Halawa* (Red and Sweet) in 1917. Meanwhile, he met playwright Badie Khairi, who became his longtime collaborator. Their work together included the plays *Talateen Yom Fil-Sign* (Thirty Days in Jail) and *Hassan wa Morcos wa Cohen* (Hassan, Morcos, and Cohen).

Al-Rihani made his first cinema appearance in 1931, in a silent film entitled *Saheb al-Sa'ada Kishkish Bey* (His Excellency Kishkish Bey). His first talking film was *Yacout Effendi* (1934). *Salama Fi Kheir* (Salama in Prosperity, 1937) was the first of a series of six films that made him one of cinema's immortals: *Si Omar* (Mr Omar, 1941); *Li'bat al-Sit* (The Woman's Game, 1946); *Ahmar Shafayef* (Red Lipstick, 1946); *Abu Halmous* (1947); and *Ghazal al-Banat* (The Flirtation of Girls, 1949). Al-Rihani himself did not live to see *The Flirtation of Girls*, a musical featuring Layla Murad at her peak, but it has since become a cherished part of the cinematic heritage.

These last films show the influence of Charlie Chaplin, who helped al-Rihani to shed the mask of Kishkish Bey and create a new character. He now became the downtrodden but eloquent and talented man, always supporting the poor against the rich; at times brave, at others a coward; forever drawn to adventures that bring only trouble, but emerging victorious; always seeking the pleasures of life, and convinced that women are the greatest of those pleasures.

Ismail Yasin (1912–1972)

Ismail Yasin belongs in the company of French comedian Fernandel, the Italian Toto, and the American Buster Keaton as a symbol of innocent laughter.

Yasin's career began when he left his home in Suez. His father had died and he ran away from his abusive mother. He had six pounds in his pocket, which he stole from under his grandmother's mattress. In Cairo, he rented a room in the poor neighborhood of Sayyida Zaynab where, by all accounts, he slept on a bed of old newspapers.

Yasin thought he sang as beautifully as Muhammad Abd al-Wahab. He sang at weddings and parties, but had trouble getting much further. Far from handsome, his face was dominated by an enormous mouth. In one of his early unsuccessful attempts to find a job in cinema, Yasin went to director Togo Mizrahi, who asked him if he had a mirror. Yasin said he did. "Have you looked at yourself?" asked the director. "How do you think you look?" "God created and God messed up!" said Yasin.

Mizrahi told him he was unfit for cinema because his face was all mouth, and suggested going to see a surgeon to make it smaller. Yasin actually did this, and although the surgeon promised to make his mouth three centimeters smaller, the operation was never performed because the fee was thirty pounds and Yasin only had ten piasters. By keeping it the way God had created it, Ismail Yasin made his mouth the most famous in Egypt.

His first film was *Khalf al-Habayib* (Behind the Lovers, 1939). Shortly afterwards, despite the mouth, Mizrahi gave him a role in *Ali Baba wal-Arba'een Harami* (Ali Baba and the Forty Thieves, 1942). He continued acting until *al-Raghba wal-Daya'* (Desire and Loss, 1972), a hundred and sixty-six films in all.

His real breakthrough was in 1949, when he starred in *al-Nasih* (The Smart One). Until then his appearances had been limited to just a few minutes, but with *The Smart One*'s success, producers were eager to give him substantial roles, and there were times when he was working on six films at once. A series of films was made with his full name in the titles: *Ismail Yasin in the Fleet, Ismail Yasin in the Police, …in the Air Force, …in the Army, …in the Zoo, …in Prison, …in the Lunatic Asylum,* and so on. Perhaps his most famous and funniest film was *Miss Hanafi* (1954), in which he played the title role.

Ismail Yasin died in May 1972, penniless, pursued by the tax authority, and banned from television. Many thought he would quickly be eclipsed by the new generation of comedians, but his films continue to draw audiences, both young and old.

Amina Rizq (1910–)

Amina Rizq's acting career has spanned seven decades. In 1924, she and her aunt Amina Muhammad, also an actress, left Tanta, their provincial hometown. Rizq settled in Cairo, joined the Ramses Troupe and has since continued her acting career uninterrupted. Her first appearance in film was in the silent feature *Suad al-Ghagariya* (Suad the Gypsy, 1928). Her most recent appearance was in the 1996 film *Nasser 56*.

Rizq never married and says she has no regrets. As she tells it, she has devoted herself to an art that dazzled her from the beginning. She was, however, closely linked to Yusef Wahbi in the first two decades of her career. She describes him as a "great pioneer and teacher." Because the two were together for so long, the public believed they were married, or at least lovers. They collaborated in many of Wahbi's plays and his early films, starting in 1932 with *Awlad al-Zawat* (Children of the Aristocracy), the first Egyptian talkie and only Rizq's second film, and ending with *Sa'at al-Sifr* (Zero Hour) in 1938. With the exception of the first film, which was directed by Muhammad Karim, all their films were directed by Yusef Wahbi himself.

With the exceptions of Yusef Chahine and Tawfik Salih, Amina Rizq has worked with all the great directors of Egyptian cinema. They saw in her face a strong peasant beauty which expressed the grace of Egyptian womanhood. She has a grasp of popular consciousness, imbued with an ennobling sadness that has only become richer over the years.

Even in her youth she played mothers, and did it so well that she became the standard for the role. One of the most important of these performances was in *Ard al-Ahlam* (Land of Dreams, 1993), where, as mother of Fatin Hamama, she outshines even that great star.

Yusef Wahbi (1897–1982)

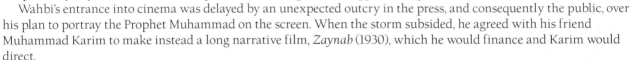

*B*orn the son of a pasha, Yusef Wahbi was expected to become an engineer like his father. But a passion for acting drove him along an unforeseen path. To his father's astonishment and rage, Yusef joined the circus. In so doing he became a person whose testimony was inadmissible in court, and a disgrace to the family. His father expelled him from the family home, then enrolled him in agricultural school in an attempt to reform him.

Wahbi fled to Italy, and plunged himself into the theater, changing his name to Ramses. He only returned to Egypt when he heard of his father's death. Even shared out between him and his four siblings, the pasha's legacy gave him personally some LE10,000 in gold. With this money, Wahbi set out to extricate the theater from what he saw as the abyss created by the dancing whiskers of Naguib al-Rihani's Kishkish Bey and the jiggling eyebrows of Ali al-Kassar.

To this end, he formed a theater company, the Ramses Troupe. In this early stage of his career, he became known as the Messenger of Divine Mercy for the Salvation of Acting. Opinion differed over the sobriquet's creator, whether it was the publicity boys of the Ramses Troupe, or the boasting and self-aggrandizing Yusef Wahbi himself.

Wahbi's entrance into cinema was delayed by an unexpected outcry in the press, and consequently the public, over his plan to portray the Prophet Muhammad on the screen. When the storm subsided, he agreed with his friend Muhammad Karim to make instead a long narrative film, *Zaynab* (1930), which he would finance and Karim would direct.

With characteristic self-confidence, Wahbi then asked Karim to direct the first Egyptian talkie. Wahbi wrote the script and played the leading role. When the film, *Awlad al-Zawat* (Children of the Aristocracy, 1932), achieved enormous success, Wahbi's confidence grew further. He wrote the script to *al-Difa'a* (The Defense, 1935), his second film, and co-directed it with Niyazi Mustafa. For his third film, *al-Majd al-Khalid* (Immortal Glory, 1937), Wahbi was author, lead actor, and director, all in one.

On three films—*Layla Mumtara* (A Rainy Night, 1939), *Layla Bint al-Rif* (Layla, Girl of the Country, 1941) and *Layla Bint al-Madaris* (Layla the Schoolgirl, 1941)—he collaborated with Togo Mizrahi, submitting his own script and role to the other man's direction. After the success of these three films, Wahbi directed *Gharam wa Intiqam* (Romance and Revenge, 1944), in which, at the age of forty-six, he played a young lover, with singer Asmahan in her second and last film, shortly before her death by drowning. The film contained a song which glorified the Egyptian royal family, and as a token of appreciation for this gesture he was awarded the title of Bey. Later, after the revolution, he received the National Appreciation Prize and an honorary doctoral degree

In *al-Iskandariya Layh?* (Alexandria Why? 1979), he played an intellectual Jew who loved Egypt, the first actor to take such a role since the Free Officers' Revolution. Wahbi was also responsible for building Ramses City, a cinematic town with a studio on more than two feddans.

Layla Murad (1918–1995)

Layla Murad began her film career in 1932, singing "The Day of Departure" in *al-Dahaya* (The Victims), directed by Badr Lama. Egyptian cinema was on the threshold of sound. *The Victims* had originally been made as a silent film, but the public wanted Hollywood-style talkies, so Lama added the song by Layla Murad. She was only fifteen.

At the time, she was being trained by Dawud Husni and her father, Zaki Murad, both prominent Jewish composers. Several years passed without further involvement in cinema, until in 1938 she was chosen to play the female lead in *Yahya al-Hubb* (Long Live Love), alongside Muhammad Abd al-Wahab. Murad combined physical grace, a sweet and well-trained voice, a beautiful face, and eyes that shone with innocence and passion. A star was born.

Togo Mizrahi swept her up and made her into the number one Egyptian actress, through four films: *Layla Mumtara* (A Rainy Night, 1939), *Layla Bint al-Rif* (Layla, Girl of the Country, 1941), *Layla Bint al-Madaris* (Layla the Schoolgirl, 1941), and finally *Layla* (1942). Then, once again, Murad disappeared from the screen, this time to reappear two years later in her fifth and final Mizrahi film, *Layla fil-Zalam* (Layla in the Dark, 1944).

The use of Murad's name in all these titles—indirectly in *Rainy Night* (Arabic for "night" is *layla*, pronounced the same as the name, but spelled differently)—shows just how marketable she was. *Layla*, her fourth Togo Mizrahi film, ran for twenty-two weeks.

Murad later married Anwar Wagdi, actor, director, and producer, converting to Islam in the process. Of the twenty-one films she went on to make, the most famous is *Ghazal al-Banat* (The Flirtation of Girls, 1949), directed by Wagdi, in which she starred opposite Naguib al-Rihani. Another great performance was in *Shati' al-Gharam* (Romance Beach, 1950), directed by Henry Barakat. Her worst film was probably her last, *Al-Habib al-Majhoul* (The Unknown Lover, 1955), directed by Hasan al-Sayfi. With the failure of this film, the banning of "With Unity, Order, and Work"—her song to commemorate the Free Officers' revolution of 1952—and the outbreak of the Suez War in 1956, Murad retired, at the age of thirty-eight.

Anwar Wagdi (1904–1955)

Anwar Wagdi was of Syrian origin, the son of a textile trader, and believed from an early age that he resembled the American actor Robert Taylor. His first appearance on stage was in *Julius Caesar* in 1922. It was not until ten years later that he made it onto the screen, taking minor parts in *Awlad al-Zawat* (Children of the Aristocracy, 1932),m then in *al-Difa'a* (The Defense, 1935).

For his part in *The Defense*, Wagdi was paid six pounds, which he spent on three tailored suits, firmly believing that his tailor would play a major role in his success.

After moving between various theater companies, he settled with the National Theater Troupe established by the government in 1935, earning three pounds a month. Over the next five years, he took leading roles in several plays. But soon cinema called him back, and he played the lead role in *Bayya' al-Tufah* (The Apple Seller, 1943), directed by his friend Husayn Fawzi. In 1944 Togo Mizrahi gave him the principal part in *Kadhb fi Kadhb* (Lies in Lies). Costarring with dancer Biba Ezz al-Din, he played a despondent young man weighed down by debt.

In 1945, he resigned from the National Theater Troupe and formed his own film company. Its first production, that same year, was *Layla Bint al-Fuqara'* (Layla, Daughter of the Poor), which he directed and starred in opposite Layla Murad. Soon after, he married Murad, and directed her in *Qalbi Dalili* (My Heart is my Guide, 1947), *'Anbar* (1948), and in 1951 his masterpiece, *Ghazal al-Banat* (The Flirtation of Girls).

In the meantime he had discovered the child actress Fayrouz, who sang and danced like an Arab Shirley Temple. He made several successful films with her, notably *Yasmin* in 1950.

By the 1950s, Anwar Wagdi had become the leading light of Egyptian cinema. His name had only to appear on a project for distributors to flock to finance it. His speciality was melodrama mixed with fast-paced musical scenes, greatly helped by the editing skills of Kamal al-Shaykh and others.

Suddenly at the height of his fame, wealthy and married to actress Layla Fawzi, Anwar Wagdi died of kidney failure, aged fifty-one.

Farid al-Atrash (1907—1974) & Asmahan (1912—1944)

Children of a Druze Prince, Farid and Amal al-Atrash arrived in Egypt with a brother and their mother, Princess Aliya, seeking refuge from the war against French occupation in Lebanon.

Their mother, herself an excellent player of the oud (Arab lute), entrusted their musical education to two of Arabic music's greatest figures, Dawud Husni and Farid Ghusn. Ghusn recognized and encouraged in his namesake a brilliance in composition and mastery of the oud. Husni renamed Farid's sister Asmahan, after a legendary Arab singer of the past.

Asmahan's creative career lasted just seven years, but in that time her reputation in the world of song grew to the point that Muhammad Abd al-Wahab saw her as the female talent to be his partner in cinema, asking her to play the female lead in *Yawm Sa'id* (Happy Day, 1939). Reluctant to actually appear on the screen, she turned the part down, but her voice can be heard in one of the scenes, singing "Qays wa-Layla."

Within two years, however, she had overcome her fear of the camera and appeared with her brother Farid in their first film, *Intisar al-Shabab* (The Triumph of Youth, 1941), the first musical to be a major success without featuring Muhammad Abd al-Wahab or Umm Kulthum. The film was directed by Ahmed Badrakhan, who soon married Asmahan in a union that lasted forty days. This was her second marriage; the first was to her cousin, Prince Hassan al-Atrash.

Between *The Triumph of Youth* and making her last film, *Romance and Revenge* (1944), released shortly after her death, Asmahan traveled to Lebanon and Syria, where she is said to have worked as a spy for the Allies. She also returned to her first husband, then divorced him again.

In order to return to Egypt, she married an unknown Egyptian singer, Fayed Muhammad Fayed, in a marriage of convenience that lasted twenty days. While shooting *Romance and Revenge*, she married producer-director-actor Ahmed Salem. This was another brief episode, which ended with Salem attempting to murder her. Soon after, she died, drowned in a Nile canal, en route to her summer home. *Romance and Revenge* appeared after her death, and became an unprecedented box-office hit.

Asmahan's brother Farid, the closest artist to her, composed a large number of her songs, including all those in *Romance and Revenge*. After her death, he lived unmarried for some thirty years. When he died in 1974, he left behind thirty films, whose directors included Henry Barakat and Yusef Chahine. In some, he costarred with Samya Gamal, principal rival to Tahiya Karioka in oriental dance. The success of his films, produced over a quarter of a century, was due not so much to their subject matter or the quality of acting—which was generally poor—as to the brilliance of their songs and dance routines.

Tahiya Karioka (1915—)

Born Badawiya Muhammad Karim Ali Sayed, Tahiya Karioka renamed herself after the Latin American "karioka" dance that Fred Astaire and Ginger Rogers had popularized in the 1933 film *Flying Down to Rio*.

A talented oriental dancer, Karioka learned her trade from the Lebanese-born cabaret queen, Badia Masabni, proprietor of Cabaret Badia, on the bank of the Nile where the Cairo Sheraton now stands. Karioka quickly became Egypt's premiere dancer. In 1936, King Faruq chose her to dance in his wedding procession.

Karioka's first appearance in cinema was a small role in the 1935 film *Doctor Farhat*. Most of her early film appearances featured only a single dance, and little notice was taken. Even before cinema, it was obligatory for performances to include both a song and a dance, a convention derived from nineteenth-century theatrical productions, particularly in France, where a light ballet was often inserted between the acts of an opera.

From the 1930s to the 1990s Karioka appeared in over 200 films. By the mid-1950s, she was typecast as a *femme fatale*. In the roles of her mature years, the overriding image is that of the *muallima*, the talented, wily woman, mistress of the scene, to whom men are always attracted. Karioka played the role on the screen and in her private life. Conservative estimates suggest she married twelve times. In an interview she described her former husbands as a bunch of philanderers.

Perhaps her best role as a dancer and *muallima* was in *Li'bet al-Sit* (The Woman's Game, 1946), in which she starred with the greatest comedian of her time, Naguib al-Rihani. She plays a young dancer who toys with men, but whose family try to exploit her by marrying her off to a rich man. Her only recourse is flight.

In the 1960s, Karioka started to put on weight, eventually reaching more than a hundred kilograms. Consequently her film roles changed from elegant dancer to older woman. She now wears the veil, a long black robe, and answers only to "hagga," a form of respectful address used for people who have performed the pilgrimage to Mecca.

Asya (1912–1986), Ahmed Galal (1897–1947), & Marie Queenie (1916–)

Asya, Marie Queenie, and Ahmed Galal were a moving force in Egyptian cinema from its very early days, and founders of a tradition carried on by blood and marriage.

Asya Dagher came to Egypt from Lebanon in 1922, dreaming of the silver screen. She started as an extra in *Layla* (1927). Just two years later, she had produced and starred in her own production, *Ghadet al-Sahara* (Flower of the Desert, 1929), the film which launched her seventeen-year career, ending in 1946 with *al-Hanem* (The Lady).

Flower of the Desert opened on 1 May 1929, featuring Asya, Ahmed Galal, and Asya's niece, Marie Queenie. This trio was to be pivotal in the film industry until 1940, competing all the while with another threesome, the Lama Brothers (Ibrahim and Badr) and Badreya Rafat. Badr died at the age of thirty-nine and Ibrahim, after killing his wife, committed suicide.

From *Ghadet al-Sahara* until *Fata Mutamarrida* (Rebellious Girl, 1940), the trio participated in every production of Asya's company, Lotus Films, with the exception of *Wakhz al-Dameer* (Pangs of Conscience, 1931), directed by Ibrahim Lama, with Galal working on the script and helping with direction. For all the other films, Galal directed and the first leading role was taken by the producer-aunt. The parts, and the films, were tailored for women as indicated by the titles: *Indama Tuhib al-Mar'a* (When The Woman Loves, 1933), *Ayun Sahera* (Bewitching Eyes, 1934), *Shagaret al-Dur* (1935), *Zawga bil-Niyaba* (The Substitute Wife, 1936), and *Fattish 'an al-Mar'a* (Search for the Woman, 1939).

Fata Mutamarrida was the first film Asya produced without appearing in it herself. The lead part was for a young woman, and taking the second role would have required Asya to play the part of a mother, thus indicating she was past her prime. Even without her, the film was a resounding success. In its wake came the announcement of Queenie's marriage to Ahmed Galal, despite the considerable age difference.

Asya and Galal continued to work together, producing two films without Queenie, who was busy producing her son Nader, who later became a director like his father and, indeed, his uncles, Husayn Fawzi (1904–1962) and Abbas Kamel (1911–1985).

Finally, a dispute broke out between Asya on one side, and Galal and Queenie on the other. The partnership was dissolved and a new company formed, Galal Films (1942), then Galal Studios (1944). Galal died of a heart attack while vacationing with his family in Lebanon in 1947. Queenie, widowed at a young age, devoted herself to production and acting and raising her son, who was to carry on the family tradition.

Henry Barakat (1914—1997)

From the age of ten Henry Barakat watched a movie every sunday at an open-air cinema under a bridge in the neighborhood of Shubra. He was besotted. All that changed over time was the setting: the Olympia in Ataba Square and the Ideal in Abdin instead of his old haunts in Shubra.

When Barakat graduated from law school, his brother decided to produce a film, *Antar Effendi*, and Barakat was assigned to supervise the shooting. As soon as Barakat entered the studio, he was gripped by the magic of blending reality and imagination. His future, he now knew, would be in film making and not in court.

As with directors Salah Abu Sayf and Kamal al-Shaykh, Barakat started his cinema career as an editor. His first editing job was in *Intisar al-Shabab* (The Triumph of Youth), directed by Ahmed Badrakhan in 1940. A few months later, he was promoted to assistant director for *al-Zawg al-Khamis* (The Fifth Husband, 1941) by Ahmed Galal. The same year, he directed his first film, *al-Sharid* (The Fugitive), adapted from a story by Anton Chekhov. Since then, Barakat has never stopped directing movies.

Like American director George Cukor, Barakat has a marvelous ability to bring out the best in his female protagonists. The performances of his favorite female star, Fatin Hamama, testify to his talent. She was at her best in films like *Du'aa al-Karawan* (Call of the Curlew, 1959), adapted from a novel by Taha Hussein; *al-Bab al-Maftuh* (The Open Door, 1963), from a story by Latifa al-Zayat; and *al-Haram* (The Sin, 1964), from a story by Yusef Idris.

The Open Door is set in the city. The heroine, by involving herself in politics and joining university demonstrations against the authorities and the occupation forces, wins her freedom. *The Call of the Curlew* and *The Sin* take place in the countryside, and both films depict the oppression of peasants with an honesty that was rare in Egyptian cinema.

In *The Sin*, Barakat shows the life of migrant workers in the Egyptian countryside. A young worker gets pregnant out of wedlock, and fearing disgrace she induces abortion. The film closes with her death, driven out of her village with incomparable cruelty. *The Sin* was shown in Cannes to great acclaim. Had this been the only film Barakat made, it would have been sufficient to mark him out as one of Egypt's greatest directors.

Fatin Hamama (1931–)

Fatin Hamama discovered the cinema when she was young, living with her family in the eastern Delta, where her father worked as a primary school secretary. Her father took her to see her first film in the provincial town of Mansura. The actress Asya was there for the opening of her new film. Young Fatin saw her from a distance, glittering in the lights, surrounded by the admiring crowd, and was captivated.

Around the same time, her father entered her for a magazine beauty contest for children. Fatin won the contest, and her father won the cash prize. Her winning picture soon found its way into the hands of director Muhammad Karim, who saw in it a delicacy he wanted for a young girl's role in his next film with Muhammad Abd al-Wahab. The film, *Yawm Sa'id* (Happy Day), was released in 1940 and when audiences left the theaters, the talk was not of established stars but about the young girl who said to Abd al-Wahab, "Mama cooked some apricot preserves for you today."

Hamama grew up in the industry and married in it, twice—first to director Ezz al-Din Zulfiqar, then to actor Omar al-Sharif—before finally marrying a respected radiologist, Dr. Muhammad Abd al-Wahab.

She was especially loved by the middle-class girls of Egyptian society, even Arab society, because in almost one hundred films she created the image of the good girl, whose fate was always in the oppressive hands of others. Her character was essentially passive, never struggling against challenges, but facing them instead with a forbearance that bordered on surrender. Her films were overwhelmingly melodramatic, to the extent that she became known as *Madame Melo*.

Despite the huge number of tear-jerkers she appeared in, her image was redeemed by a sharp intelligence. She was leading lady in Henry Barakat's best films: *Du'aa al-Karawan* (Call of the Curlew, 1959), *al-Haram* (The Sin, 1965), *al-Khayt al-Rafi'* (The Thin Thread, 1971), and *La Azza' lil-Sayidat* (Women Can't Come to the Funeral, 1979). In the 1993 she appeared in Dawud Abd al-Sayed's *Ard al-Ahlam* (Land of Dreams), which, despite its box-office flop, is considered by many one of the best films of the decade.

Omar al-Sharif (1931–)

Omar al-Sharif was born Michel Dimitri Shalhoub, to an Alexandrian family of Lebanese descent. He was discovered by director Yusef Chahine, who cast him in three films: *Sira'a fil-Wadi* (Feud in the Valley, 1953), *Shaytan al-Sahara* (The Desert Devil, 1954), and *Sira'a fil-Mina* (Feud in the Port, 1955). The friendship with Chahine soured however, and all cooperation between them ended after *Feud in the Port*.

A passionate love affair with star Fatin Hamama led to marriage, following her divorce from director Ezz al-Din Zulfiqar.. Several films later, in some of which he costarred with his wife, including *Ard al-Salam* (Land of Peace, 1955) by Kamal al-Shaykh and *La Anam* (I Don't Sleep, 1957) by Salah Abu Sayf, he was chosen by French director, Jacques Baratier, to star in *Goha* (1958).

Until 1963, when David Lean cast him as Sharif Ali in *Lawrence of Arabia*, he acted only in Egyptian films, some now classics: *Ihna al-Talamiza* (We are the Students, 1959) by Atef Salem, *Bidaya wa Nihaya* (A Beginning and an End, 1960) by Salah Abu Sayf, and *Fi Baytuna Ragul* (A Man in Our House, 1961) by Henry Barakat.

With his nomination for an Oscar as best supporting actor in *Lawrence of Arabia*, Omar al-Sharif became an international star, and for over twenty years he acted only in foreign films, with one exception, *al-Mamalik* (The Mamelukes, 1965) by Atef Salem. He appeared in *The Fall of the Roman Empire* (1964) by Anthony Mann, *Dr Zhivago* (1965) by David Lean, and *Funny Girl* (1968) by William Wyler.

From 1969, his acting career went downhill, and he began to accept minor parts in poor films. Finally he returned to Egypt and made four films: *Ayyoub* (1984) and *al-Aragoz* (The Puppet, 1989), both TV productions directed by Hany Lasheen; *Muwatin Misri* (Egyptian Citizen, 1993) by Salah Abu Sayf; and *Dihk wa Li'b wa Gad wa Hubb* (Laughter, Play, Seriousness, and Love, 1993), Tarek al-Tilmissani's first film.

None of these films achieved the success worthy of Omar al-Sharif's status in Egyptian cinema as its only actor to rise to international stardom. But, alongside the best of his films, his dashing good looks and his skill at bridge ensure that he is not forgotten.

Abd al-Halim Hafiz (1929—1977)

For thirty years, Muhammad Abd al-Wahab dominated Arabic song. Then suddenly a sickly young man called Abd al-Halim Hafiz appeared, and earned for himself the name *al-Andalib al-Asmar*, The Dark Nightingale.

The upstart's sudden rise to fame took the Singer of Kings and Princes by surprise. In an attempt to smother him, he signed him up with his own production company, *Sawt al-Fann* (The Voice of Art) and paid him a pittance. But there was no stopping the new arrival, and before long he was every girl's dream and the role model for young men. He had replaced Abd al-Wahab in their hearts.

His success was even enough to irritate Umm Kulthum. "Boy, you're a crooner, not a real singer," she told him one day, in front of the press.

In his short life, Abd al-Halim made more films than Abd al-Wahab and Umm Kulthum put together, acting and singing with almost every female star of the 1950s and 1960s. He shared his first film, *Lahn al-Wafa'* (The Song of Fidelity, 1955) with Fatin Hamama and singer Shadia. In *Banat al-Yawm* (Today's Girls, 1957), he costarred with actress Magda, and in *al-Wasada al-Khaliya* (The Empty Pillow) with Lubna Abd al-Aziz. Mariam Fakhr al-Din played alongside him in *Hikayat Hubb* (Tale of Love, 1959), followed by Suad Husni in *al-Banat wal-Sayf* (The Girls and Summer, 1960), and Zubayda Tharwat in *Yawm min 'Umri* (A Day in My Life, 1961). In *al-Khataya* (The Sins, 1962) he was joined by Nadia Lutfi, who appeared with him once again in 1969 in *Abi Fawqa al-Shagara* (My Father is up the Tree).

Henry Barakat, who directed him in *Ayyam wa-Layali* (Days and Nights, 1955), *Maw'id Gharam* (A Romantic Date, 1956) and *Today's Girls* (1957), described Abd al-Halim as "sensitive, as much an actor as he was a singer." Other directors who helped his ascent to stardom were Muhammad Karim in *Dalila* (1956), the first Egyptian film in cinemascope; Salah Abu Sayf in *The Empty Pillow* (1957); Hilmi Rafla in *Fata Ahlami* (Man of My Dreams, 1958) and *Ma'budat al-Jamahir* (Public Idol, 1967); Fatin Abd al-Wahab in *The Girls and Summer,* Hasan al-Imam in *The Sins* and Husayn Kamal in *My Father is up the Tree*.

My Father is up the Tree, Abd al-Halim's last film, was an unprecedented success in Egyptian cinema, running for thirty-six weeks. Abd al-Halim played the lover of a prostitute (Nadia Lutfi) in a tavern on the Alexandria harbor. His rival is his father, played by Emad Hamdi. Young men would return to the theater several times in an effort to count the kisses. The film has never been shown on Egyptian television, for censorship reasons.

Na'eema Akef (1929–1966)

Na'eema Akef's father owned the Akef Circus and at the age of four, she began her training as a trapeze artist. Growing into a beautiful young woman, she became an oriental dancer at Casino Badia Masabni. She made a brief dancing appearance in *Sit al-Bayt* (Lady of the House, 1949) by Ahmed Kamel Morsi.

Soon after, director Abbas Kamel saw her dance at a night club and was so taken by her that he quickly brought his brother, Husayn Fawzi, to the club. As soon as he saw her, Husayn felt he had found what he was looking for, a girl with a talent for dancing, singing, acrobatics, and acting, and with a beautiful face and gorgeous figure. He gave her the lead role in his film *al-Eish wal-Malh* (Bread and Salt, 1949), opposite singer Saad Abd al-Wahab, Muhammad Abd al-Wahab's nephew. Audiences immediately fell in love with her and fame was instantaneous. Husayn Fawzi quickly monopolized her, signing her up for his coming films.

Their relationship culminated in marriage although Husayn was almost twenty-four years older. Na'eema's first eleven films were all directed by Husayn Fawzi, who also wrote the script for most of them—that remains unique in Egyptian cinema, and perhaps in any cinema in the world.

After starring in *Arba' Banat wa Dhabit* (Four Girls and an Officer, 1954) by Anwar Wagdi, Na'eema took the lead role in Fawzi's *Bahr al-Gharam* (Sea of Love, 1955) opposite Rushdi Abaza. Then she made *Madraset al-Banat* (The Girls' School, 1955) with Kamel al-Tilmissani. Before their divorce, she made two more films with Husayn Fawzi: *Tamr Henna* (Tamarind) and *Ahebak Ya Hassan* (I Love You Hassan), both in 1957.

Altogether Na'eema Akef and Husayn Fawzi made fourteen successful films, all comedy-musicals revolving around a high spirited, common girl: a showgirl with whom the pasha's son falls in love in *Lahaleebo* (The Firebrand, 1949); an alley girl who rejects the pasha's temptation in *Baladi wa Khifa* (Common and Light, 1950); a street girl finding work for her family in a theater in *Furigat* (Relief, 1951); a circus girl with whom an aristocrat falls in love in *Fatat al-Sirk* (Circus Girl, 1951); a club dancer who discovers the barman is her father in *al-Nimr* (The Tiger, 1952). Once they divorced, both stars began to wane. Husayn Fawzi died in 1962, and Na'eema four years later, aged just thirty-seven.

Suad Husni (1943–)

*A*fter she first appeared in Henri Barakat's *Hassan wa Na'eema* (Hassan and Na'eema, 1959), Suad Husni became known as the Cinderella of the Screen and The Mischievous Girl. Born into an artistic family, she started her career at the age of three. She could act, sing, dance, and perform both comedy and tragedy; a woman with a thousand faces and beautiful eyes.

However, for more than eight years, she too often appeared in films by second or third-rate directors, or directors who were past their prime.

In 1966, she costarred with Rushdi Abaza, an actor of amazing presence, in *Shakawet Rigala* (Men's Mischievousness) by Hossam al-Din Mustafa, *Saghira ala al-Hubb* (Too Young to Love) and *Ganab al-Safir* (His Excellency the Ambassador) by Niyazi Mustafa, and *Mabka al-'Ushak* (Lovers' Wailing) by Hasan al-Sayfi. Famous directors like Salah Abu Sayf, Kamal al-Shaykh, Yusef Chahine, Hassan al-Imam, and Atef Salem competed for her. Ahmed Badrakhan ended his career with Suad starring in his film *Nadia* (1969).

Al-Qahira Thalatheen (Cairo '30, 1966), adapted from a story by Naguib Mahfouz, and *al-Zawga al-Thaneya* (The Second Wife, 1967) from a story by Ahmed Rushdi Saleh were Abu Sayf's most successful films with Suad Husni. In 1979, Husni played a Persian spy in the Iraqi propaganda film *al-Qadisseya*, Abu Sayf's worst film, shown only in a second-rate theater in Cairo.

Yusef Chahine directed her in *al-Ikhtiar* (The Choice, 1971) from a story by Mahfouz and *al-Nass wal-Nil* (The People and the Nile, 1972) about building the Aswan High Dam. Neither achieved any success, and the second was a disaster.

Her three films with Kamal al-Shaykh—*Bi'r al-Hirman* (Well of Deprivation, 1969), *Ghurub wa Shuruk* (Sunset and Sunrise, 1970) and *Ala Man Nutlik al-Rassass* (Who Do We Fire At?)—were hugely successful. Her film with Atef Salem, *Ayna Akli?* (Where's My Mind? 1974) achieved similar success.

Her finest moment, however, was in Hassan al-Imam's musical melodrama, *Khalli Balak min Zuzu* (Watch our for Zuzu, 1971). For the first time in Egyptian cinema, Suad played a mischievous university student who initiates the flirting with her beau, until he falls in love with her. Its success is perhaps only matched by *Abi Fawqa al-Shagara* (My Father is up the Tree).

At the peak of her glory, she married Ali Badrakhan, son of the director of *Nadia*. During their marriage and after their divorce and her marriage to scriptwriter Maher Awad, he directed six of her films, from *al-Hubb iladhi Kan* (The Love That Was, 1973) to *al-Ra`i wal-Nissa'* (The Shepherd and the Women, 1991) with which she ended her career at the age of forty-eight.

Rushdi Abaza (1927–1982)

Born of an Italian mother and an Egyptian father, Rushdi Abaza was the scion of a respectable old family whose members held high posts in the state. As a student at St. Mark's College in Alexandria, Rushdi was fonder of body building and athletics than academic studies. He was well-proportioned and muscular, with a handsome face radiating Egyptian and Roman blood. He captivated the camera immediately and it remained his captive for over a quarter of a century.

Abaza stepped directly into cinema without any stage experience. His performance was therefore purely cinematic, unaffected by the theater, unlike stars such as Yusef Wahbi, Yahya Chahine, and Shoukri Sarhan.

His debut was in a small role in *al-Millionaira al-Saghira* (The Little Millionairesse, 1948) starring Faten Hamama and directed by Kamal Karim.

It was two Italian directors, Alessandrini and Virenco, who first gave Abaza prominent roles: in Alessandrini's *Amina* (1949) and Virenco's *Imra'a min Nar* (Woman of Fire, 1950) and *Sham al-Nessim* (1952: the title is the name of an old Egyptian festival)., Egyptian directors failed to realize that a star had been born who could, if properly handled, elevate Egyptian cinema. For over seven years, they only gave him unimportant minor roles, as a playboy or villain. Finally Husayn Fawzi chose him for lead roles opposite Na'eema Akef—then at her peak—in *Bahr al-Gharam* (Sea of Love, 1955) and *Tamr Henna* (Tamarind, 1957). Top directors soon began to compete for Rushdi.

Among his important films at the time were Kamal al-Shaykh's *Tuggar al-Mawt* (Merchants of Death, 1953), and Ezz al-Din Zulfiqar's *Tariq al-Ammal* (The Road of Hope, 1957) and *Imra'a fil-Tariq* (Woman on the Road, 1958).

With fame came a flood of offers; in a single year (1960), he starred in eleven films. In 1961 he was chosen by Abbas Kamel for *H-3* (1961) opposite Suad Husni. This film was the first of twelve that Abaza and Husni made together over a period of thirteen years, ending with Atef Salem's *Ayna Akli?* (Where's My Mind? 1974).

As he approached fifty, Abaza's health deteriorated, as did his films. From the last seven years of his life, perhaps only two films will be remembered: *Ureedu Halan* (I Want a Solution, 1975) by Barakat and *Alam Iyal fi Iyal* (A World of Kids, 1975) by Muhammad Abd al-Aziz.

He died in 1982 before completing *al-Aqweya'a* (The Strong).

Salah Abu Sayf (1915–1996)

Cairo is the capital of the cinema industry in the Arab World. It could not have attained this status without pioneers like Salah Abu Sayf. Starting out as an editor, he went on to directing films for over fifty years.

His movies have two distinctive characteristics: unity of space and unity of dramatic treatment. Three quarters of his movies take place in Cairo. Through them one can construct a record of much of Cairo's social history. The space in which his characters move is Cairene: the public bath in *Laka Yawm ya Zalim* (Tyrant, Your Day Will Come, 1951) and *Hamam al-Malatili* (The Bath House of Malatili, 1973); the Zamalek quarter in *Osta Hassan* (Foreman Hassan, 1952); the Citadel district and the neighborhood of Abbasiya in *Shabab Imra'a* (A Woman's Youth, 1956); Shubra in *Bidaya wa Nihaya* (A Beginning and an End, 1960); and the vegetable market of Rod al-Farag in *al-Fitiwwa* (The Tough Guy, 1957).

All his films refer in some way to Islam, the religion of most Cairenes. With the exception of two films with non-Muslim protagonists, all his characters, despite their differences, are Muslims.

In the work of Abu Sayf, Cairo's omnipotence, and its social distortions—marked by misery and the attempt to escape it—produce a disfigurement in human relationships, which can lead to tragedy. With only a few exceptions, his films revolve around this deformity and its consequences. Migration from the countryside to the metropolis is the subject of *A Woman's Youth, The Tough Guy,* and *The Bath House of Malatili;* movement from one neighborhood to another is the subject of *Foreman Hassan, La Waqt lil-Hubb* (No Time for Love, 1963), and *A Beginning and an End*. The path of Abu Sayf's characters, as they try to force their way up from their low social status, rarely changes. Although it is defined by three interrelated issues—livelihood, sex, and knowledge or freedom—the basic motive is always to confront poverty. Fear of poverty and the attempt to escape it are the recurring themes of his films. Abu Sayf's cinema about the popular quarters of Cairo expresses a profound understanding of these neighborhoods and the people who live there.

Kamal al-Shaykh (1919–)

Kamal al-Shaykh decided early on that his life was to be in films, and not, as his parents hoped, in law. On the advice of director Muhammad Karim, he tried to get involved with Studio Misr. A government minister who lived near his family in Helwan gave him an introduction to the poet Khalil Motran, then director of the Cairo Opera, who in turn recommended him to Ahmed Salem, Studio Misr's director. Three months later he was taken on, but spent his first year in the editing department doing very little. Over the next ten years, however, he edited a great many films, including such landmarks of Egyptian cinema as *Ghazal al-Banat* (The Flirtation of Girls, 1949) and *Shati' al-Gharam* (Romance Beach, 1950). The experience prepared him for his first film as director, *al-Manzal Raqam Thalath 'Ashar* (House No. 13, 1952).

Until he stopped directing after the failure of *Qahir al-Zaman* (Conqueror of Time, 1987), a science fiction feature, al-Shaykh worked constantly, sometimes against the prevailing current, to avoid what he saw as the banality and sloppiness that characterized Egyptian cinema all around him. Dances and songs were only used where dramatically necessary, dialogue was never overblown, and the action never descended into farce or slapstick. Actors were carefully chosen for specific roles, and never employed just because they were box-office stars.

Al-Shaykh was greatly influenced by Alfred Hitchcock. In his third film, *Haya aw Mawt* (Life or Death, 1953), a little girl buys medicine for her sick father, but after she leaves the pharmacy, the chemist realizes he has mistakenly given her poison. The race that ensues between life and death is a brilliant example of al-Shaykh's mastery of suspense.

Among his finest achievements are two films based on novels by Nobel Prize winner, Naguib Mahfouz: *al-Liss wal-Kilab* (The Thief and the Dogs, 1962) and *Miramar* (1969). With the exception of Salah Abu Sayf's *A Beginning and an End* (1960), none of the tens of other films based on stories by Mahfouz rises to the level of *The Thief and the Dogs* or *Miramar*—testimony to a director who believes that cinema is high art.

Tawfik Saleh (1927—   )

In a career in cinema of more than forty years, Tawfik Saleh has made just seven feature films. *Al-Mutamarridun* (The Rebels, 1967) was banned for political reasons, and his last two films, *al-Makhdu'un* (The Dupes, 1972) and *al-Ayyam al-Tawila* (The Long Days, 1980), made in Syria and Iraq, have never been shown in Egypt.

In Saleh's last year at university, Tawfik al-Hakim's play, *Russassa fil-Qalb* (A Bullet in the Heart) was presented at the French Friendship Club in Alexandria. Saleh was asked to direct it just three days before its presentation. The French Cultural Attaché was impressed by Saleh's direction and sent him to study theater in Paris for a year.

Saleh returned to Egypt soon after the Free Officers' revolution, having actually studied cinema rather than theater. His first film, *Darb al-Mahabil* (Fools' Alley, 1954) was influenced by *al-Suq al-Sawda'* (The Black Market, 1943), which Saleh had seen being filmed by director Kamel al-Tilmissani during his first year at university. *The Black Market* was set in a poor district of Cairo in the manner of director Kamal Selim's *al-Azima*, but unlike *al-Azima*, this time there was no happy resolution at the hands of an enlightened pasha. Instead, the people confronted the greedy merchants and emerged victorious. With this setting in mind, Saleh collaborated with Naguib Mahfouz, in his first work for cinema, to create a film which was outside the ordinary in every respect. Although awarded the National Prize for Directing in recognition of its social commentary, *Fools' Alley* was badly received by both critics and public.

Saleh then made no films for seven years, until 1962, when he directed *Sira'a al-Abtal* (Conflict of Heroes), relating the cholera epidemic of the 1940s to the effects of British occupation. Over the years, he made three more films, *The Rebels*, based on a story by journalist Salah Hafiz; *Yawmiyat Na'ib fil-Aryaf* (Diary of a Country Prosecutor, 1968) from a novel by Tawfik al-Hakim; and *al-Sayyid al-Bulti* (Mr Bulti, 1969) from a story by Saleh Mursi.

He then moved to Syria for four years, where he made his masterpiece, *The Dupes,* written by Palestinian author Ghassan Kanafani about the tragedy of the Palestinian diaspora.

In 1973, Saleh moved to Iraq, directing his last film, *The Long Days*, about Saddam Husayn's revolutionary youth. He now lives in Cairo.

Niyazi Mustafa (1911—1986)

Niyazi Mustafa lived with Egyptian cinema for over half a century—from its birthing pains in the mid-thirties until 19 October 1986, when he was found murdered in his apartment, a crime that remains unsolved to this day.

The brighter side of Mustafa's love story with cinema started when he persuaded his father to send him to study engineering in Germany. Once on German soil, he switched to the Cinema Institute in Munich.

After graduation, he trained at UFA Studios in Berlin (1932), then worked as assistant to German director Rupert Volmut. On his return to Egypt, he worked as assistant director to Yusef Wahbi on *The Defense* (1935).

His next move was to Misr Company for Acting & Cinema, where he made documentaries about Banque Misr companies. One of these, *Suq al-Milah* (Market of the Handsome, 1936), was a song and dance sketch, featuring Badía Masabni and her troupe, among whom was Tahiya Karioka, who was to become Egypt's greatest oriental dancer in the forties and fifties.

When Studio Misr was built, Mustafa was appointed chief editor and supervised the production of the early issues of the Egypt Newsreel. He was also responsible for the editing of *Widad* (1936) and *Lasheen* (1939), both directed by the German Fritz Kramp.

His first feature film, *Salama Fi Kheir* (Salama in Prosperity, 1937), showed his considerable talent and grasp of cinematic language, and marked him out as an important figure in the industry. Meanwhile, he had married his assistant editor, Kouka, and he gave her the lead role in *Masna'a al-Zawgat* (The Wives' Factory, 1941). She also starred as the bedouin girl in *Rabha* (1943), *Antar and Abla* (1945), and *Raweya* (1946).

With the exception of two comedies, *Salama Fi Kheir* and *Si Omar* (Mr Omar, 1941), both featuring Naguib al-Rihani, top comedian of the day, and both extremely successful, his early films had provocative social messages, beginning with *al-Doktor* (The Doctor, 1939), then *Madraset al-Zawgat* (School for Wives) and *Wadi al-Nugum* (Valley of the Stars) in 1943. When these three films had no success while cheap action films and musicals by lesser directors were attracting audiences in droves, Niyazi opted for pure commercialism. He began with *Rabha* then *Taqiyet al-Ikhfa'* (The Invisible Cap) where, with a budget of just LE8,500, he employed special effects with a dexterity none could match. Even with a cast of then only second-tier stars (Muhammad Kahlawy, Tahiya Karioka, and Bishara Wakeem), the film was a box-office hit, earning some LE250,000, a huge figure at the time.

Given impetus by this success, Niyazi went on to become a director unrivaled for the size and variety of his output. His last film, *al-Koradaty* (The Monkey Trainer, 1986), had as its only star a monkey called Simsim. Niyazi himself was murdered before he finished editing the film.

Hassan al-Imam (1921—1988)

When Hassan al-Imam graduated in 1936 from the Frères school in Cairo, he joined the Ramses Troupe, apprenticing himself to its owner, Yusef Wahbi. Limited to small roles on stage, he also wrote lyrics for Thoraya Hilmi, which she sang in Badia Masabni's cabaret, and radio operettas like *Laylat Masra' Kiliyubatra* (The Night of Cleopatra's Assassination) and *Min Irtah?* (Who was comforted?)

With the theater recession during the Second World War, al-Imam gravitated to cinema, working as assistant director to Ahmed Galal, Niyazi Mustafa, and Yusef Wahbi.

The high-pitched melodrama that marks most of al-Imam's work was clearly announced in his first film, *Mala'ika fi Jahanam* (Angels in Hell, 1946). His films were enormously successful and his repute spread, particularly as a director of weepies. In imitation of Alfred Hitchcock he took to making a brief appearance in all his films.

Al-Imam made several films about famous bellydancers. He began with Shafiqa al-Qubtiya (*Shafiqa the Copt*, 1963), followed by *Imtithal* (1972), *Bint Badia* (Wonderful Girl, 1972), *Bamba Kashar* (1974), *Badia Masabni* (1975), and *Sultanat al-Tarab* (The Sultana of Song, 1979).

One of his most successful films was *Khalli Balak min Zuzu* (Watch out for Zuzu, 1972), with script and songs by poet and cartoonist Salah Jahin. The plot revolves around a university student (Suad Husni), with whom a fellow student from a respected family (Husayn Fahmi) falls in love. When he discovers Zuzu's mother is a bellydancer, complications begin.

Al-Imam also made a number of films based on the novels of Naguib Mahfouz, beginning with *Zuqaq al-Midaq* (Midaq Alley, [1963), with scenario and dialogue by policeman-turned-writer Saad al-Din Wahba. Its success encouraged al-Imam to film Mahfouz's *Trilogy*—for which Mahfouz won the Nobel Prize for literature—*Bayn al-Qasrayn* (Palace Walk, 1964), *Qasr al-Shawq* (Palace of Desire, 1967), and *al-Sukkariya* (Sugar Street, 1973), with scenario and dialogue by another policeman-cum-author, Mamduh al-Laythi, winner of the National Prize for Literature.

Regrettably, the films, although commercially successful, were cheap caricatures of the author's *Trilogy*, depriving it of its depth and rich characterization. With the failure of his last film *Dunya Allah* (God's World, 1975), another Mahfouz story, al-Imam returned to playing small parts, notably in Ali Abd al-Khaliq's *Madafin Mafrusha lil-Igaar* (Furnished Tombs for Rent, 1986).

Fatin Abd al-Wahab (1913—1972)

All but seven of Fatin Abd al-Wahab's fifty-seven films were comedies, the harvest of a cinematic career that began in 1949 with *Nadia*, and ended in 1972 with *Adwa' al-Madina* (City Lights), which was first shown two months after his death.

In 1939, Fatin graduated from War College and joined the military, remaining in service until 1954. In the meantime, he also had a life in cinema. In 1945, he worked with Yusef Wahbi as a production assistant, then as assistant director to Ezz al-Din Zulfiqar.. There were some striking similarities between Fatin and Ezz al-Din. Both were army officers, both expressed themselves through cinema, and both were from artistic families. Fatin's brothers were director Hassan Abd al-Wahab and actor Sirag Munir, husband of actress Mimi Shakib. Ezz al-Din's brothers were actor and director Mahmud Zulfiqar, husband of actress Aziza Amir, and actor Salah Zulfiqar. Both Fatin and Ezz al-Din married stars: Fatin married Layla Murad, whom he divorced after she bore his only son Zaki, another actor and director. Ezz al-Din married Fatin Hamama and divorced her after she gave birth to their daughter Nadia, who was given a rather unsuccessful role in one of her mother's films.

Fatin's first comedy was *al-Ustadha Fatima* (Professor Fatima, 1952), in which Fatin Hamama played her first comedy role. From 1954, Fatin's name became attached to comedian Ismail Yasin. That year, he directed *al-Anisa Hanafi* (Miss Hanafi), in which Yasin plays a man who turns into a woman on his wedding night and marries a butcher. With the film's success, the following years saw an intense collaboration between Fatin and Yasin, with six films in the famous series *Ismail Yasin in...* (*Ismail Yasin in the Army, Ismail Yasin in the Police*, and so on).

In the early 1960s, Fatin's work took a new turn, and a vein of social criticism appeared in his comedies. *Al Zawga al-Thalitha 'Ashr* (Wife No. 13, 1962), *Ah Hawa* (Oh Eve, 1962), *'Arus al-Nil* (Bride of the Nile, 1963), *Mirati Mudir 'Amm* (My Wife the General Director, 1966), and *Ard al-Nifaq* (Land of Hypocrisy, 1968) made Fatin the most important Egyptian director of comedy.

Shadi Abd al-Salam (1930–1986)

Shadi Abd al-Salam marked himself out from all other Egyptian film makers by a fierce love of ancient Egyptian history. Ironically, in the early years it was only foreign companies that allowed him to express this fascination. In 1960 he was chosen to design the pharaonic boat used in the American film *Cleopatra*, and in 1967 to design sets and the pharaoh's costumes in the Polish film *Pharaoh*. He then met Italian director Roberto Rosselini, who hired him to design costumes and sets for one part of *Struggle for Survival*, a serial about ancient Egypt. Without this experience he could never have produced his two masterpieces: *Al-Mummiya* (The Mummy, 1969; also known as *The Night of Counting the Years*) and *Shakawi al-Fellah al-Fasih* (Complaints of the Eloquent Peasant, 1970). Both films are classics of Egyptian cinema—extraordinary works in a film industry remarkable for its neglect of everything connected to ancient Egypt.

The Complaint of the Eloquent Peasant, based on the record of a pharaonic papyrus, is just twenty-three minutes long and is produced with a precision that borders on the miraculous.

The Mummy takes its inspiration from the discovery near Thebes in 1882 of a hidden cache of royal mummies. Some three thousand years before, the remains of more than forty royal mummies of various dynasties had been hastily reburied to protect them from tomb robbers. The film presents a complex set of symbols about the problems of modern Egypt, its relationship with its pharaonic past, its perspective on the West, and its Arab identity.

In 1974 Abd al-Salam wrote a script about the tragedy of Akhenaton, the "accursed" monotheist pharaoh, to be called *Tragedy of the Big House*. However, following the critical success of his first two films, Abd al-Salam's enemies went to great lengths to prevent his new script from appearing on the screen. Abd al-Salam died having directed only one long narrative film. Jean Lescure, chairman of the French Cinema Union, said, "For us Egyptian cinema starts with *The Mummy*, and if conditions prevail, cinema historians will assume its death with it too."

Yusef Chahine (1926—)

Yusef Chahine, internationally known through the films he has shown at festivals, particularly Cannes, is the most famous of Egyptian directors at home and abroad.

Son of Lebanese Maronite parents who settled in the Alexandria of Lawrence Durrell, Chahine was educated at Victoria College, Egypt's elite school of the time. After graduating, he traveled to the United States, where he studied drama at UCLA. He returned to Egypt in 1948, and directed his first film, *Baba Amin* (Father Amin) in 1950. His second film *Ibn al-Nil* (Son of the Nile) went to the 1951 Cannes film festival.

In the first fifteen years of his career he directed sixteen feature-length fiction films. Most were comedies or straightforward commercial melodramas—with two important exceptions: *Bab al-Hadid* (Cairo Station, 1958) and al-*Nasir Salah al-Din* (The Victor Saladin, 1963). In the first film Chahine plays a crippled, mentally unstable newspaper vendor who is not taken seriously as the suitor of a beautiful girl who sells cold drinks—the sex symbol Hind Rustom. *Saladin*, one of the first Egyptian color films, is an epic account of the struggle between Arabs and Crusaders in Palestine.

After directing *Fagr Yom Gadid* (Dawn of a New Day, 1965) for the public sector, Chahine moved to Lebanon where he made one documentary and two narrative film. *Bayya' al-Khawatim* (The Ring Seller, 1965), starring Lebanese singer Fayrouz, was Chahine's simplest and most romantic work. However, the attempt to move the center of cinema production to Lebanon failed, and Chahine returned to Egypt, to work again in the government-controlled public sector. In 1972 he made *The People and the Nile*, in celebration of the Aswan High Dam, and *Al-Ard* (The Land, 1970) about the struggle of peasants against feudalists. *The Land* entered the competition in the 1969 Cannes festival before its release in Cairo.

With *al-'Usfur* (The Sparrow, 1973), Chahine's films assumed a political and historical character, a tendency that was to increase over time. Most were French co-productions, often with Francophone leanings, even celebrating France's cultural role in Egypt's history in *Adieu Bonaparte* (1984), which entered the Cannes competition the following year.

Chahine is the only Egyptian director to have made autobiographical films. His first, *al-Iskandariya Layh?* (Alexandria Why? 1979), won the special jury award in Berlin in 1979. He took his autobiography to the cinema again in *Hadouta Masriya* (An Egyptian Tale, 1982) and in *al-Iskandariya Kaman* (Alexandria Again, 1989). On the fiftieth anniversary of the Cannes festival the jury presented Chahine with a special prize in recognition of his work.

Supporting Stars

Soliman Naguib (1890-1955)

Zuzu Shakib (1909-1978)

Bishara Wakim (1891-1949)

Said Abu Bakr (1913-1972)

Abd al-Fattah al-Qosari (1905-1965)

Muhammad Kamal al-Masri (Sharafantah) 1886-1958

Riyad al-Qasabgi (1902-1963)

Mahmud Shoukoukou (1912-1985)

Widad Hamdi (1924-1994)

Mimi Shakib (1913-1982) & Estefan Rosti (1891-1964)

Salah Nazmi (1918-1991)

Sirag Munir (1901-1957) with Mimi Shakib

Abd al-Salam al-Nabulsi (1899-1968)

Nigma Ibrahim (1910-1976)

Soraya Fakhri (1914-1965)

Elwiya Gamil (1910-1994) & Zaki Rostom (1903-1972)

Zenat Sidki (1913-1978)

Aziz Osman (1893-1954)

Mahmud al-Meligi (1910-1983)

Husayn Riyad (1897-1965), Mimi Shakib & Abbas Fares (1902-78)

Hassan Fayeq (1897-1980) & Said Abu Bakr (1913-1972)

Fardos Muhammad (1906-1961)

Fuad Shafiq (1899-1962), Mary Monib (1905-69) & Camilia